The forgotten art of fighting against multiple opponents

A Practical Guide for Staff and Baton Martial Artists

by
Luís Franco Preto
MSc in Sports Training Sciences

To Master Nuno Curvello Russo
**A brilliant martial artist and fierce fighter whose skills
and knowledge will probably be appreciated only after he is gone,
like it has been with so many others before him in all walks of life.**

The forgotten art of fighting against multiple opponents
A Practical Guide for Staff and Baton Martial Artists

by
Luís Franco Preto
MSc in Sports Training Sciences

Copyright 2014 ©

Cover design & illustrations by Danai Vlachou

ISBN-13:978-1500465094
ISBN-10:1500465097

All rights reserved. No part of this publication may be reproduced or transmitted in any form or in any means, electronic or mechanical, including photocopying, recording, or any information storage and retrieval system known or to be invented, without permission of the author in writing, except by a reviewer who wishes to quote brief passages in connection with a review written for inclusion in a magazine, newspaper or broadcast or upon the World Wide Web.

Luís Franco Preto (1978 -)
Neither the author nor the publisher assumes any liability for the use or misuse of information contained in this book, nor does the author or publisher encourage the use of Martial Arts' techniques other than for personal development and historical study. Study of historical Martial Arts can be dangerous and should only be practiced under the guidance of a qualified instructor.

Acknowledgements

I would like to extend a heartfelt thanks to the following people for their help in gathering the photos for this book:
- Andy Fosmark
- Frederico Martins
- Julia Dordel
- (Master) Nuno Mota
- Roland Cooper
- Devon Boorman who, not only participated in the photo shooting, but also generously allowed the use of the training facilities of Academie Duello.

Table of contents

Introduction 13
    Understanding the history behind the development of the skills of the art **17**
    Self defence oriented philosophy **17**

SECTION ONE:
Theoretical principles 21

Putting theory into practice 25
Engaging multiple opponents 27
    Awareness **29**
    Engagement through distance management **30**
        • Phase one **31**
        • Phase two **34**
    Understanding the premise behind this tactic **38**

SECTION TWO:
Techniques of combat against multiple opponents 41
Technique I – Sweep from above 43
    Staff **45**
    Baton **53**
        • Sweep from above on non dominant side **53**
        • Sweep from above on dominant side **55**
    Application of the sweep from above against two opponents **57**
        • Phase one **57**
    Lining up opponents **64**
        • Phase two **68**

Practical settings of engaging multiple opponents 71
    Staff **73**
        • Scenario A **74**
        • Scenario B **84**
    Baton **92**
        • Adjusting footwork **92**
        • Adjusting striking technique **96**

Technique II – The backward sweep **109**
   Staff **111**
      • Step one **111**
      • Step two **111**
      • Step three **111**
      • Step four **118**
      • Step five **118**
   Baton **122**
      • Option A **122**
      • Option B **126**
   Application of the backward sweep in combat against two opponents **130**
   Staff **130**
   Baton **136**
      • Phase 1 **137**
      • Phase 2.i **142**
      • Phase 2.ii **145**
   Adding a follow through strike **150**

SECTION THREE:
Combat against three opponents **157**
Combat against three opponents **159**
   Overall guidelines on positioning **161**
   Staff **162**
      • Step one **162**
      • Step two **166**
      • Step three **172**
      • Step four **180**
      • Step five **183**
   Baton **186**
      • Step one **186**
      • Step two **190**
      • Step three **194**
      • Step four **195**

Special Notes **197**
   The historical link to single combat **199**

Final Notes **210**

About the author **212**

"There's a difference between interest and commitment.
When you're interested in doing something,
you do it only when circumstances permit.
When you're committed to something,
you accept no excuses, only results."
~ Art Turock

Introduction

Introduction outline

Understanding the history behind the development of the skills of the art
Self defence oriented philosophy

> *"Does history record
> any case in which
> the majority was right?"*
> ~ Robert Heinlein

IN MY OPINION, A BOOK ON JOGO DO PAU and the system of this Portuguese staff fencing art for fighting against multiple opponents is equivalent to a book on the origins of European Historical Fencing. The reason I claim this is because I consider that Jogo do Pau and Historical Fencing are one and the same thing. I base this conclusion on the following:

1) There are Portuguese documents which allow us to conclude that, as long sword medieval fencing systems were replaced within the military by firearms, they were kept alive by civilians through the use of staffs. I myself am also capable of performing the exact same skills with both weapons. Thus, the first conclusion we can draw is that:

> **The categorization of
> Jogo do Pau
> as a Portuguese staff-only fencing system
> is incorrect.
> Jogo do Pau is actually
> a medieval fencing skill set
> which was historically applied
> to both long swords and staffs,
> depending on the social factors
> that determined which weapons
> were available.**

2) Before the recent focus on the development of the combat sport 'Canne de Combat', France had its own "staff fencing" art which, interestingly enough, was named "Jeux du Baton"- which is French for Jogo do Pau! Nuno Curvello Russo, who is regarded as the most experienced and knowledgeable Jogo do Pau instructor in Portugal, lived in France during the seventies, where he met Maurice Sarry. Like Russo, Sarry had dedicated himself to the in-depth study of the traditional fighting art of his country, and he was highly regarded on a national level. As these two great masters got acquainted with one another, they

decided to train together. Shortly after, they realized that all the traditional techniques for dueling that made up the two arts were absolutely identical (I am specifically referring to dueling technique because at the time, the French art had become exclusively focused on this type of combat, just like it had happened with Jogo do Pau in the urban industrial cities of Portugal). Hence, the second conclusion we can draw is that:

> **Jogo do Pau is not merely a Portuguese fencing art, but a European fencing art. Consequently, this means that European Fencing is Jogo do Pau**

Please note that I do not wish to sound disrespectful towards other European systems, such as the German and Italian. Though they are also European Historical Fencing, I consider that just like it happens with other motor activities, there is one common set of technical foundations that can be used under different tactical perspectives - that is the element responsible for bringing about distinct styles. Thus, the "European Historical Fencing style" of Jogo do Pau gathers a set of guiding principles on universal concepts such as distance, timing, parrying and striking angles – to name just a few – that characterize both its specific practice as well as European Historical Fencing as a whole.

Furthermore, I consider that this specific topic of combat against multiple opponents represents the origin of Historical Fencing given that:

> As a whole, the martial methods around the world have their roots in the development of the ability to fight against multiple opponents. Military conflicts that took place in the Middle Ages involved large armies that collided in the battlefield., This means that soldiers had to be ready to fight many opponents approaching simultaneously from different directions. Without a doubt, the origin and essence of martial arts lies in the development of effective combat skills that will allow a fighter to overcome such scenarios. Even within civilian environments, the most common self defense situation entails having to defend against multiple opponents who wish to steal one's assets. In this sense, we can safely assume that the development of combat skill within European fencing arts was just like in Jogo do Pau, initially focused on the study of technical and tactical skills that address the challenges of combat against multiple opponents.

At the same time, combat against multiple opponents happens to be one of my favorite topics in martial arts. In absolute honesty, having practiced Asian martial arts under circumstances that only had me dealing with imaginary opponents, having to manage real opponents was one of the main things that attracted me to Jogo do Pau. In this regard, I find that a large part of the martial arts world lacks understanding on this subject and that a little insight could go a long way. Hence, it is with an enormous passion and feeling of relevance towards this topic that I will present the concepts of Jogo do Pau on outnumbered combat.

Understanding the history behind the development of the skills of the art

Before actually analyzing the specific motor skills regarding the concepts of Jogo do Pau for combat against multiple opponents, there is one historical element that needs to be clarified: the art was born and developed way before the Industrial Revolution took place, meaning that most people still lived in rural environments where they:

1) Carried long walking staffs that were extremely useful for combat, in the absence of swords

2) Most often there was no shortage of space to swing such weapons, which explains the strong reliance of the system on wide-arc striking motions

Consequently, it is only natural to start this analysis of outnumbered combat as a "product" of the historical factors that shaped the art, by focusing initially on the use of long double handed weapons.

However, since Portugal also went through the Industrial Revolution, the relatively recent development of cities brought about the replacement of the traditional walking staff by the walking cane, and the subsequent adaptation of the double-handed weapon techniques of the art to shorter – one-handed – weapons. Therefore, over the course of this book, I shall also address the methods and skills of combat against multiple opponents using a single-handed weapon which, although similar to those of the staff, have some particularities which need to be addressed separately.

In the last section I shall explain how combat against multiple opponents and one-on-one combat are historically and technically connected and how the skills of the former influenced the development of skills of the latter. It is my hope that you enjoy reading this book and that it will influence your martial training by making it even more interesting and enjoyable.

Self defence oriented philosophy

I find that for people to really understand martial arts from a combat perspective, it is useful to draw a parallel between combat and the art of trapeze.

Over time, the introduction of safety nets has significantly changed the conditions under which trapeze artists perform. The introduction of this piece of equipment makes its practice much safer and reduces the psychological stress levels experienced before each performance.

Personally, I consider the preparation of martial artists for self defense combat the development of the ability to fight without a safety net, regardless of whether one is facing one or ten opponents. Sometimes, one opponent can even turn out to be more dangerous than ten, not only because of his skill level, but also because he does not split his attention between reading his opponent and coordinating himself with his "mates".

The all too common myths of unbeatable combat systems and foolproof techniques that are often propagated by contemporary martial arts have little (if any) similarity with the cruel and ugly reality of actual violence, therefore, the first guideline of combat against multiple opponents is the following very simple rule:

The only foolproof strategy that will guarantee one's safety is to avoid being involved in physical conflicts altogether. Consequently, people should try to avoid conflicts and, whenever that fails, they should first and foremost try to escape.

For a number of reasons, there are cases when escape will not be possible and the only available option will be to fight. Whenever that occurs, it is crucial that people fight to win by not holding anything back! Nevertheless, I have known a few individuals who deliberately look to fight so as to feed their ego, which results in having them unnecessarily adding more wood to a fire that could, and should, be put out using simpler and safer strategies. Ultimately, these people end up fighting more often than needed and, consequently, many end up either dead or in prison, meaning that:

**Avoidance and running away whenever possible
is just a matter of being smart,
not a sign of weakness!**

Ultimately, this philosophical discussion boils down to the choice between "living to fight or fighting to live". However, as I pointed out before, there will always be some situations in which fighting is unavoidable and, very often, while having to face a higher number of opponents. Thus, let us proceed with the analysis of the specific techniques and strategies that offer combatants the best chance for overcoming such challenges.

SECTION ONE

Theoretical principles

FIGHTING AGAINST ONE OPPONENT OF THE SAME SKILL LEVEL is a dangerous scenario in which combatants have at best a fifty percent chance of an outcome that will be considered successful. Thus, when fighting against multiple opponents, the chances for a successful outcome decrease with every new opponent that is added. Obviously, this makes avoidance and escape strategies much more valid options than engagement with the opponents. In case the way to escape is blocked, here are some basic considerations in order to manage the opponents while still looking for a way to escape.

Are opponents positioned at a distance which makes them an immediate threat? Baring the use of projectiles, opponents who are standing at a distance of five meters, for example, will first have to close the distance in order to perform any type of attack with either their limbs or striking weapons.

Images 1 & 2: Combatants positioned at a distance outside the reach of their weapons

This means that whenever combatants are able to keep their opponents at a distance they will, at least, avoid getting hit. Consequently:

The strategy of a combatant who is outnumbered must be to keep opponents at a distance while looking for an opening to escape.

At the same time, the outnumbered combatant should try to take advantage of mistakes the opponents might make, by striking them. However, an opponent's mistake is only a bonus and it should be treated as such. It is very dangerous to approach outnumbered combat expecting to out-strike multiple opponents, because it will most probably place the outnumbered combatant in unfavorable situations.

We will now proceed and break down how this strategy can be implemented.

Putting theory into practice

Engaging multiple opponents

chapter outline

Awareness
Engagement through distance management
- Phase one
- Phase two

Understanding the premise behind this tactic

Awareness

Every martial system is based on certain principles in order to be effective. Although these principles may vary somewhat between systems, there is one which I consider universal, and that is awareness.

Unfortunately, it is more common for people within the martial arts community to focus on training for impossible or near impossible scenarios than on learning how to prevent them. Unfortunately, real violence has very little to do with what we see in martial arts films, which is often perpetuated by numerous instructors. To put it simply:

**You should,
first and foremost,
try to prevent and avoid conflicts
and physical altercations!**

If you neglect awareness and avoidance and train with the mentality that bad situations are inevitable, chances are that you will end up facing one. However, real violence turns out to be a very hard reality check for most people, when they realize that overcoming the odds against non compliant opponents is not as easy as it seemed in practice.

Thus, awareness should be the first and universal principle in all martial systems. If you consistently allow yourself to be caught off-guard by attackers, you will always have to beat the odds in order to win a fight, and you will not survive for long. In order to have a good chance of successfully overcoming multiple opponents, you must first detect them, preferably at a distance. Otherwise you will end up being ambushed and, unless your opponents are complete amateurs or idiots, the outcome will not be favorable.

Now, although awareness can and SHOULD be trained, its training methodology is outside the scope of this book. I will assume then, that trainees are already able to exercise this skill, and will proceed directly to the actual combat methodology of Jogo do Pau.

Engagement through distance management

PHASE ONE

Position yourself at a distance between five and ten meters from your training partner. The one designated as the attacker, must approach and deliver a strike by taking several approaching steps while holding his weapon in a forward pointing waiting guard position. As the front tips of the weapons are about to touch, the attacker should perform one final approaching step at the same time he is performing a strike.

Starting from a distance outside the reach of the weapon, the attacker has to close the distance before performing a strike (Double handed weapons)

Engaging multiple opponents • 31

During this first practice phase, the "defender" should not move, so as to allow the attacker to land a controlled strike thus providing the attacker with visual feedback at the end of the strike regarding the spatial management of this technique.

**Starting from a distance outside the reach of the weapon, the attacker has to close the distance before performing a strike
(Single handed weapons)**

PHASE TWO

Repeat the same exercise but as the attacker is closing the distance, the defender will focus on detecting when the attacker starts performing the last approaching step while he is still in a waiting guard stance. As the attacker starts that final stepping motion in a waiting guard, the defender should release a strike of his own while stepping forward at the same time.

In this exercise, the defending partner learns how to manipulate the distance so as to perform a pre-emptive strike that takes the attacker by surprise as he is approaching. This way, the attacker is forced to assume a defensive and reactive mindset.

Performing a pre-emptive strike against an approaching opponent (Double handed weapons)

The way to engage multiple opponents (assuming that the combatant has detected them from a distance) is by using pre-emptive strikes that will momentarily place attackers in a defensive mindset.

Performing a pre-emptive strike against an approaching opponent (Single handed weapons)

Engaging multiple opponents

Understanding the premise behind this tactic

By remaining at a distance from the opponents, the outnumbered combatant forces – or lures – them to close the distance themselves. This way, the outnumbered combatant is able to turn these conditions to his advantage by performing a pre-emptive strike that places his opponents in a defensive and reactive role.

This is the main guiding principle that combatants should adhere to when engaging multiple opponents. However, before putting it to practice, trainees need to become acquainted with the main technique which is to be performed both afterwards and, sometimes, during the actual initial engagement phase.

Luring in opponents so as to force them into a defensive and reactive role

Engaging multiple opponents · 39

SECTION TWO

Techniques of combat against multiple opponents

Technique 1 – Sweep from above

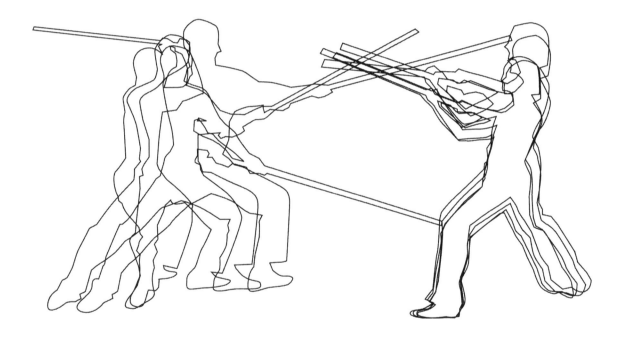

chapter outline

Staff
Baton
- Sweep from above on non dominant side
- Sweep from above on dominant side

Application of the sweep from above against two opponents
- Phase one

Lining up opponents
- Phase two

Sweep from above

STAFF

Students work in pairs: one student positions his weapon forward and upward so as to simulate an incoming strike. The other places his dominant leg forward and the weapon pointing backwards, while slightly above his head on his non dominant side.

From this position, trainees extend their upper limbs forward, so as to use both weapons to visually gauge the distance from their partner.

After adjusting the distance, trainees

Standard initial stance

Measuring the initial distance from which to start this exercise

return to the previously described overhead backward pointing waiting guard in order to practice the sweep from above.

The sweep from above consists of two actions performed consecutively. The first is a half rotational oblique descending strike, meant to sweep the opponent's weapon to the side. This is followed by a second strike, a full rotational one, towards the opponent's body.

The initial half rotational strike should be performed without stepping forward, since the goal is to simply intercept the opponent's weapon,. and this can be performed from the initial position.

Upon completing this movement, the weapon does not stop, but continues in a full rotational strike on the same side. This time the target of the technique is the opponent's body, so a full approaching step will be necessary.

In the initial stages of this exercise, the training partner providing the target stays at the same spot. In later stages, the partner providing the target will first retreat out of striking distance and, later, retreat and parry the strike.

First phase of the sweep from above

Technique I – Sweep from above • 47

Second phase of the sweep from above, directing the strike towards the opponent's head or knee

Technique 1 – Sweep from above · 49

Performing the sweep from above with the opponent exiting in order to avoid getting hit (pages 48-50)

Technique 1 – Sweep from above • 51

II. BATON
Sweep from above on non dominant side:

Performing the sweep from above with the baton follows the main overall concept previously presented for the staff. Only two slight adjustments are required.

Since this is a one handed weapon, it is not possible to stop the movement of the arm in a forward extended position as the initial half rotational strike intercepts the opponent's weapon. Practitioners should allow for the baton to naturally swing upwards as they flex their arm in order to powerfully swing the weapon forward again.

Standard initial stance with the baton

Sweep from above on the non-dominant side with single handed weapons

Sweep from above on dominant side:

It is also necessary to train the same technique on the opposite side, placing the non dominant leg forward and the baton, pointing backwards on the dominant side.

This time the half rotational sweep is released on the dominant side and the counter attack on the non dominant, with the trajectories of both strikes oblique descending ones.

Sweep from above on the dominant side with single handed weapons (pages 53-54)

Application of the sweep from above against two opponents

Starting position in order to apply the sweep from above against two opponents

PHASE I

Practitioners form groups of three, with the partner practicing the sweep facing one opponent while the other stands behind him.

The outnumbered combatant performs the sweep from above against one partner, displacing his opponent's weapon with the first strike and completing the movement with the counterstrike that is performed simultaneously with an approaching step.

As depicted in the previous photos, the sweep from above allows the outnumbered combatant to push one opponent away while stepping out of the other opponent's striking reach. As the second strike lands, the outnumbered combatant should turn the head towards his dominant side, thus looking over his dominant shoulder so as to observe the opponent approaching from behind.

Sweep from above against the opponent on the right

Technique 1 – Sweep from above

As the opponent is approaching from behind, the outnumbered combatant must shift his weight towards his dominant leg, so as to perform another sweep from above.

Finishing the sweep from above while looking:
At the opponent being attacked (A)
Towards the one approaching from behind (B)

Technique 1 – Sweep from above

This will enable the outnumbered combatant to push away the approaching opponent once again, at the same time that he is able to step out of the other opponent's striking distance.

By continuously performing sweeps from above both opponents are kept at bay. However, it is easy to understand that this is more tiring for the outnumbered combatant, which is why we need to point out once again that:

Using the increased distance towards the opponent approaching from behind in order to pre-emptively strike him

Outnumbered combatants should immediately escape once they have gained the necessary space and time to do so.

Lining up opponents

One final note is probably needed concerning the well known strategy of lining up opponents.

I believe that some readers might be already criticizing the previously described engagement strategy, given that it implies having the outnum-

bered combatant placing himself between his opponents, instead of trying to line them up so as to fight one at a time.

It so happens that combatants who are truly motivated to really hurt their outnumbered oppo-

Lining up two passive opponents

nent and, once again, aren't complete idiots, will attempt to surround they "prey". Therefore, even if one does try to line them up, they will react by adjusting their positioning as well, instead of passively just allowing themselves to be lined up. This analysis and experience of how fighting really does

Lining up two non passive opponents

develop brought about the decision of channelling our tactical reasoning in the direction of developing the ability to handle the circumstance of being surrounded from the very beginning.

PHASE TWO

In combat, like in most competitive sports, speed is fundamental. Fencing arts are no different and, when combatants are forced to fight multiple opponents simultaneously, it becomes even more important.

Therefore, in order to successfully manage multiple opponents, it is necessary to improve the performance of the sweep from above by going from looking at the opponent one is attacking when finishing the sweep from above, to finishing the second strike of the sweep from above while already looking at the opponent approaching from behind. For most people, this is especially difficult to perform due to emotional constraining factors, since finishing striking techniques while looking in the opposite direction makes people quite fearful of being unable to control their strikes and, thus injure their training partners should they fail to protect themselves adequately.

Improving technique by going from finishing the first strike looking ahead (B) to being already observing the opponent(s) approaching from behind (C)

However, such a concern shows a training attitude which is, not only the opposite of what should be combatants' frame of mind, but also one that induces the development of an incorrect technique. I obviously agree that, given the special nature of these activities, training will not last if some control is not exerted on most occasions. Nevertheless, trainees are better off using simple exercises such as this one where they can safely assume that everything will turn out ok and, consequently, perform their strikes correctly by means of having them going past their opponents' bodies while already looking the other way.

If, nevertheless, some concerns do still exist during the early stages of training, it is preferable to start training slowly but correctly and, as confidence grows regarding training partners' ability to exit, slowly increase execution speed.

Practical settings of engaging multiple opponents

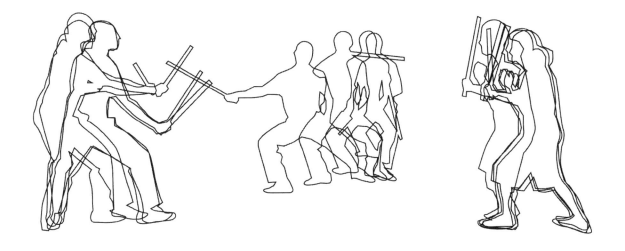

chapter outline

Staff
- Scenario A
- Scenario B

Baton
- Adjusting footwork
- Adjusting striking technique

UP UNTIL NOW, WE HAVE EXPLAINED THE MAIN PRINCIPLE of engaging multiple opponents by managing distance in a way that allows the outnumbered combatant to execute successful pre-emptive strikes. We will now proceed and describe how to actually perform this principle against multiple opponents.

Staff

When the outnumbered combatant finds himself surrounded by the opponents, he should react by positioning himself in a forward pointing waiting guard, and a stance with the non dominant leg forward. In addition to that he needs to ensure that he is facing between the opponents, not one of them, in order to have visual access to both.

**Correct (A) & incorrect (B) positioning
in order to control the approach of both opponents**

When fighting with staffs, the outnumbered combatant should:

1) Control the approach of the opponents in order to detect which one is closing the distance faster,

2) Upon determining which one is closest, perform a strike against this opponent.

This skill should be developed by practicing the following two scenarios:

SCENARIO A

As an introductory drill, as the opponent on the non dominant side approaches, the outnumbered combatant performs an oblique descending strike on the dominant side, taking a double half step towards that opponent. By performing this step, instead of a passing step (a full step forward), he can finish the initial strike without turning his back to the other opponent. In order to perform the double half step straight towards one opponent and, thus, increase the distance from the remaining

Opponent on the right approaches

opponents as much as possible:
• The rear leg is drawn behind the lead leg in the opponent's direction.
• This initial step is followed by a step with the lead leg towards the opponent.
• A third step is performed, with the rear leg crossing behind the lead leg again. This final step allows the outnumbered combatant to position himself at a better angle in order to keep all opponents in his field of view.

Incorrect execution: taking a full step forward when performing the first strike makes it harder to control and move towards the other opponent

Practical settings of engaging multiple opponents • 77

Approaching the opponent on the right with a double half step

Taking the initiative by moving the back leg behind
the lead leg, for greater stride length

Using the third step for better positioning

SCENARIO B

In this scenario, the opponent on the outnumbered combatant's dominant side approaches first.

In this case, the outnumbered combatant should lift his weapon and point it backwards on the non dominant side and perform a sweep from above.

Opponent on the left approaches first

However, due to the greater distance between the outnumbered combatant and his opponents, the sweep from above will require two full approaching steps, one with each strike.

Performing the sweep from above in other to push away the opponent on the left, while increasing the distance from the opponent on the right (see also photos on following spread)

Practical settings of engaging multiple opponents

After performing the sweep from above towards one opponent, so as to push him away and increase the distance from the second opponent, the outnumbered combatant should immediately perform another sweep from above towards the opponent approaching from behind. This will allow him to move the opponents further apart and create more space, which will increase the time available to manage them.

As the outnumbered combatant completes the first sweep from above, he must move the back leg so as to immediately square off with the other opponent and quickly follow

through with another sweep from above.

In order to get a firm grasp of these concepts, trainees should practice by alternating between taking the initiative against either opponent, in order to easily memorize these new skills.

Down the road, trainees should practice with their opponents approaching randomly, since that will force the outnumbered combatant to develop the ability to read which opponent is approaching first.

Practical settings of engaging multiple opponents

Pushing the opponent on the right away, while stepping out of the other opponent's reach

Practical settings of engaging multiple opponents

Baton

When fighting with the baton, taking the initiative against multiple opponents follows the same principles but requires a few adjustments.

ADJUSTING FOOTWORK

When fighting with batons, instead of always initiating movement with the back leg, the outnumbered combatant should start by moving the leg which is closest to the opponent who is approaching first. This means stepping with the left leg when moving to the left side and stepping with the right leg when moving to the right side.

Hence, when moving towards the side of the lead leg, the outnumbered combatants will be merely sliding the lead leg in the direction of the attacker. Therefore, he will have less reach on this side than when taking the initiative against the opponent on the side of the back leg. This should be taken into account too when determining which opponent is closest. Ultimately, this means that when fighting with the baton, the outnumbered combatant will more often than not initiate movement towards the side of the back leg. Thus, taking the initiative towards the side of the lead leg occurs only when the opponent on that side is significantly closer than the remaining ones.

Engaging the opponent on the right by sliding lead leg

Engaging the opponent on the left

ADJUSTING STRIKING TECHNIQUE

Since the baton is shorter than the staff, combat distance will also be shorter and, consequently, sparring will also be faster. Therefore, it is highly likely that the group of assailants will be approaching by being closer together, which makes it extremely difficult to initiate by performing a full double-strike sweep from above. Hence, outnumbered combatants should perform the following alternative strategies:

1) Unleash a single strike towards the first attacker that moves into striking reach and immediately follow up with a full sweep from above (two strikes) against the other opponent.

2) Perform a single strike towards both opponents, so as to push each of them a bit further away. This will obviously increase the distance between the opponents enough to allow for a full double-strike sweep from above, this time towards the opponent against whom the outnumbered combatant performed the initial strike.

These adjustments, characteristic of shorter one handed weapons, will force outnumbered combatants to be capable of performing the sweep from above on both sides.

Forcing the opponent on the right to retreat before performing a full double-strike sweep from above towards the opponent on the left (see also images on following spread)

Practical settings of engaging multiple opponents · 99

Forcing the opponent on the left to retreat before performing a full double-strike sweep from above towards the opponent on the right (see also images on following spread)

Practical settings of engaging multiple opponents · 103

Performing only one strike against each opponent before committing to the double-strike sweep from above against the first opponent (see also images on following spread)

Practical settings of engaging multiple opponents · 105

Technique 11 – The backward sweep

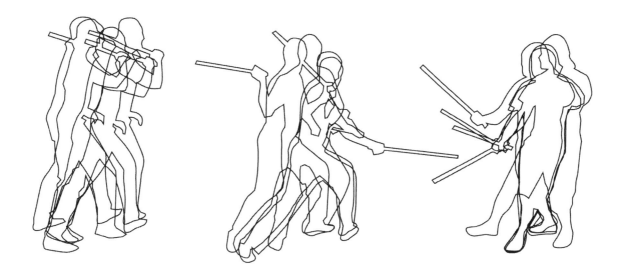

chapter outline

Staff
- Step one
- Step two
- Step three
- Step four
- Step five

Baton
- Option A
- Option B

Application of the backward sweep in combat against two opponents

Staff

Baton
- Phase 1
- Phase 2.i
- Phase 2.ii

Adding a follow through strike

The backward sweep

STAFF

Step one
From a non dominant leg lead stance, perform an oblique descending strike on the dominant side.

Step two
From the same non dominant lead leg stance, take a full step back with the lead leg.

Step three
Afterwards, perform the same back stepping technique only, this time, finishing the back step facing backwards.

Initial stance for the performance of the upcoming building steps

STEP ONE
Oblique descending strike on the dominant side

Technique 11 - The backward sweep

STEP TWO
Full backwards step

STEP THREE
Finishing the back step facing backwards

Technique 11 - The backward sweep • 117

Step four
Combine the striking technique with the back step.

Step five
Bring everything together by performing the striking technique towards the back.

STEP FOUR
Combining the striking technique
with the back step

Technique II - The backward sweep

STEP FIVE
Performing the striking technique towards the back

Technique II - The backward sweep • 121

BATON

Once again, fighting with the baton requires a few adjustments, this time regarding the backward sweep, which can be performed in two ways.

Option A

If the second strike of the sweep from above is not blocked by the opponents, both the weapon and the outnumbered combatant will naturally follow through with a rotational oblique descending strike.

Performing the sweep from above without having the second strike blocked

Technique 11 - The backward sweep • 123

As the tip of the weapon moves past the opponent, the outnumbered combatant should raise his arm above the head and take advantage of the momentum of the weapon to fluidly follow through with a backward sweep were the weapon performs a full overhead rotation.

**Following the sweep from above
with an overhead rotational backwards sweep**

Technique 11 - The backward sweep • 125

Option B

In case the opponent is able to block the second strike of the sweep from above, the outnumbered combatant will have to perform a backward sweep directly from the end position of the previous strike towards the opponent approaching from behind.

If the opponent blocks the second strike of the sweep from above, the backward sweep will be performed without any rotation

Technique 11 - The backward sweep • 127

Outnumbered combatants must practice the backward sweep with the baton on the opposite side, as was the case with the sweep from above.

**Backward sweep on the opposite side,
after having the weapon either blocked or not blocked**

Technique 11 - The backward sweep • 129

Application of the backward sweep in combat against two opponents

STAFF

When the outnumbered combatant is positioned between two opponents, he should perform a sweep from above against one opponent, a second sweep from above against the other opponent and a backward sweep against the first opponent.

The tactical purpose of this sequence is to use the sweeps from above to push one of the attackers away while immediately getting out of his striking reach. Upon finishing the second sweep from above, the outnumbered combatant will have created enough space and time in order to surprise the opponent initially attacked with a strike coming from the side opposite to that of the sweep from above.

After finishing the first sweep from above towards the opponent on the left, the outnumbered combatant should square off with the other opponent by assuming the same waiting guard (see also next spread)

Technique 11 - The backward sweep

After performing two sweeps from above, the outnumbered combatant follows through with a backwards sweep

Technique 11 - The backward sweep • 135

BATON

In order to develop the understanding and skill of how to apply the backwards sweep with the baton, the drill previously described for the staff should be practiced, but with the opponents alternating be-

tween blocking and merely avoiding the final strike of the outnumbered combatant's sweep from above. This will help trainees distinguish between the two situations and, thus, follow through with the appropriate variation of the backward sweep.

Phase 1
After using the sweep from above to push away
the opponent on the right, the outnumbered combatant
performs a second sweep from above towards
the opponent on the left
(see also the two following spreads)

Technique 11 - The backward sweep

Technique 11 - The backward sweep • 141

Phase 2A
The opponent blocks the second strike of the sweep from above, and the outnumbered combatant is forced to perform a direct backward sweep
(see also images on page 142)

Technique 11 - The backward sweep · 143

Phase 2B
The opponent evades the second strike of the sweep from above, and the outnumbered performs a rotational backward sweep (see also the two following spreads)

Technique 11 - The backward sweep • 147

Technique 11 - The backward sweep

ADDING A FOLLOW THROUGH STRIKE

After practicing the previous drill, the outnumbered combatant should practice following through the backward sweep with a second strike, which will require taking another forward step. This gives the outnumbered combatant more options and, therefore, makes him less predictable. Nevertheless, it requires being skilled in all the different variations

of the sweep from above and the backward sweep that were previously described, since this strategy forces outnumbered combatants to constantly change the side on which they hold their weapon upon squaring off with the opponent approaching from behind.

Performing a follow through strike after the backwards sweep (see also the following two spreads)

Technique 11 - The backward sweep • 151

Technique 11 - The backward sweep • 153

Technique II - The backward sweep • 155

SECTION THREE
Combat against three opponents

Combat against three opponents

chapter outline

Overall guidelines on positioning
Staff
- Step one
- Step two
- Step three
- Step four
- Step five

Baton
- Step one
- Step two
- Step three
- Step four

Overall guidelines on positioning

When fighting against three opponents, if they are skilled combatants, they will attempt to position themselves forming a triangle around the outnumbered opponent. In this case, the outnumbered combatant should keep himself outside the triangle, so as to keep all opponents in his field of view.

Incorrect (A&B) & correct (C) positioning

Combat against three opponents • 161

STAFF

Step one: When three opponents attempt to position themselves in the form of a triangle against a single opponent, the outnumbered combatant should place himself outside the triangle so that, by looking towards the centre, all opponents are kept in his field of view. Then, the outnumbered combatant should perform a sweep from above towards the opponent on his dominant side. Note that when performing the sweep from above against three opponents, the outnumbered combatant should focus his gaze towards the centre of the triangle (unlike what happened when performing the sweep from above against two opponents).

Sweep from above towards the opponent on the dominant side

By performing additional identical sequences of sweep from above towards the opponent on the dominant side and the backward sweep towards the opposite opponent, outnumbered combatants are able to apply the same principles previously explained and, therefore, successfully push one opponent away at the same time that they increase the distance from the remaining ones.

Combat against three opponents

Backward sweep towards the opponent non dominant side

Combat against three opponents · 165

Step two: The previous drill should now be repeated, with the group of assailants now actively seeking to surround the outnumbered combatant. How should the outnumbered combatant deal with this challenge?

What outnumbered combatants usually tend to do is to slightly adjust their position by stepping sideways and slightly to the back when performing the sweep from above and the backward sweep. This way they can compensate for the attempts of the opponents to surround them and

While performing the backwards sweep, the opponent previously attacked should try to move within striking distance again, and towards the outnumbered combatant's back

keep the opponents within their field of view. The problem with this tactic is that, if it is repeated multiple times, the outnumbered combatant will constantly move towards the same direction and eventually will find himself trapped against a wall or other obstacle.

A better way to solve this problem is to use the opponents' movement against them:

As the attackers try to surround the outnumbered combatant, they increase the distance between themselves. For example, after pushing away the first opponent (the one on the dominant side) with the sweep from above, the outnumbered combatant will perform the backward sweep towards the second opponent, the one on his back. At this moment, the first opponent will attempt to move towards the outnumbered combatant's back, thus increasing his distance from the third opponent, the one in the middle.

Hence, outnumbered combatants should follow through with another sweep from above towards this opponent who is approaching from behind, only by sliding their lead foot forwards before taking a full forward step with the back leg. This allows them to push the opponent back and still finish the sweep from above stepping over the imaginary line that connects that combatant with the one in the middle.

Finally, by performing a short spin, outnumbered combatants are able to maintain all three opponents in their field of view and, consequently, promptly follow through with a strike towards the opponent who was initially placed in the middle but is now approaching from behind.

By systematically repeating this strategy, outnumbered combatants will move to a different side of the triangle formed by the opponents after each backward sweep. After performing this change of position towards the dominant side for three consecutive times, outnumbered combatants will return to the side of the triangle they started from.

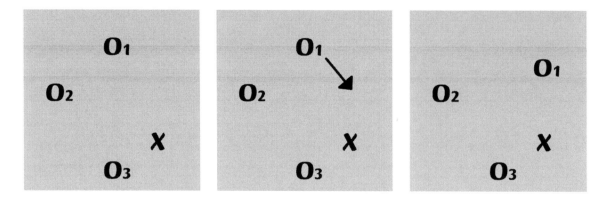

As combatant **X** performs a backward sweep towards **O3**, **O1** closes the distance, moving towards **X**'s back, which increases the distance between **O1** and **O2**

Combat against three opponents · 169

Performing a sweep from above in order to
take advantage of the opponents' surrounding motion

Combat against three opponents • 171

Step three: This time, as the opponent on the dominant side moves towards the back of the outnumbered combatant while the latter performs the backward sweep, the opponent positioned in the middle decides to move towards his partner in order to reduce the distance between them, in an attempt to make it harder for the outnumbered combatant to move to that side.

Realizing that O1's motion will open the gap between them, O2 opts to move towards O1 so as to close that gap

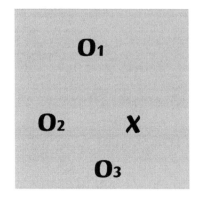
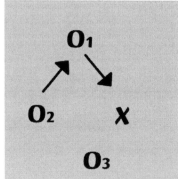
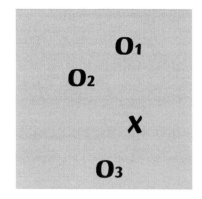

However, although this strategy closes the gap on one side, it increases the gap between the opponent in the middle and his other partner. Therefore, when the outnumbered combatant finishes the backward strike towards the opponent on his non dominant side under these circumstances, he should follow up with a sweep from above towards the opponent in the middle.

Changing sides towards the opponent in the middle
as result of the opponents' different positioning
(see also the two following spreads)

Just like in **Step two**, this sweep from above needs to be initiated by moving the dominant leg towards the opponent whom the outnumbered combatant is approaching, before performing a full step forward with the back leg. This will place the outnumbered combatant on the outside of the triangle formed by the opponents.

Additionally, upon executing the sweep from above which was used to change sides towards a different side of the triangle, outnumbered combatants should, once again, follow through with a sweep from above towards the opponent who is approaching from behind.

Given that outnumbered combatants should step towards a different side of the triangle after performing each backward sweep, upon changing sides three times by always stepping towards the opponent in the middle, outnumbered combatants will return to the side they started from.

Combat against three opponents • 177

As previously described, the outnumbered combatant should follow the change of side with an immediate sweep from above towards the opponent that was pushed away before changing sides

Step four: After getting acquainted with these two tactical options by practicing them separately, trainees should start integrating them within the same drill, which will include the following options:

1) Moving through the triangle made up by the opponents by changing sides three time clockwise followed by three counterclockwise changes.

2) Afterwards, trainees should start free sparring

with the multiple opponents moving randomly. This will require the outnumbered combatants to finish the backward sweep while already checking out the position of the remaining opponents. As the outnumbered combatant does so, he has to determine which side offers more space for him to step into and then perform a sweep from above while taking two steps towards that greater opening.

Finishing the backward sweep while already evaluating the position of the remaining opponents

Combat against three opponents

Finishing the backward sweep under different circumstances,
with the biggest opening varying according to the opponents' positions

Step five: In the most advanced stage or practice, trainees should make free sparring a bit more complex by adding the previously described skill of engaging multiple opponents. Since three opponents will give outnumbered combatants even less space to move among them, performing a first

Drawing in the opponents and taking the initiative against the one on the dominant side (see also the following spread)

sweep from above in order to immediately change sides will not be possible. Instead, outnumbered combatants need to perform the engagement technique already described earlier, starting by taking the initiative towards the opponent on their non dominant side in order to create a little more space before committing to a change of side.

From this position either perform a sweep from above while immediately changing sides (straight ahead or towards the opponent on the dominant side) or simply spread the opponents a bit more by performing a sequence of a sweep from above and a backward sweep, before eventually gathering the necessary conditions (space) to change sides.

BATON

The same concepts apply when using the baton against three opponents with just a few slight adjustments required.

Taking the initiative with single-handed weapons against the opponent on the dominant side

Step one: After practicing the training sequence previously described for the staff with single handed weapons (by performing the sweep from above on the non dominant side), trainees should practice of the exact same sequence for the sweep from above on the dominant side.

Combat against three opponents · 187

Following through by changing sides, while performing the sweep from above on the dominant side

Combat against three opponents · 189

Step two: Afterwards, trainees should introduce the following variation which is specific of the baton.

Instead of always performing the full double strike sweep from above, the outnumbered combatants should limit its use for when changing sides. After changing sides, he ought to follow up towards the opponent approaching from behind by performing only the first strike of the sweep from

above. This requires only a half approaching step towards the opponent.

This partial execution of the sweep from above allows the outnumbered combatant to quickly strike the opponent who was initially pushed away while changing sides. This strategy is fundamental in managing aggressive opponents who exert pressure much faster with these shorter weapons.

Following the change of side with a sequence of one strike towards each opponent (see also the following two spreads)

Combat against three opponents

Combat against three opponents • 193

After getting a good feel for this strategy, trainees should alternate between following their changes of side with either the full double-strike sweep from above or the first strike only. This will make it easier for trainees to retain these similar yet slightly different tactical options.

Step three: Afterwards, trainees need to repeat the previous training sequence for the sweep from above on the dominant side.

Step four: Finally, trainees should practice performing the full double-strike sweep from above mainly when changing sides, while following through the backward sweep with a second strike. Each time that the backward sweep is followed by a second strike, the outnumbered combatants will be forced to change the side on which they are performing the next sweep from above.

Special notes

WHEN FIGHTING AGAINST four opponents, they will represent the four corners of a rectangle. This will not change the strategy and techniques used by the outnumbered combatant in any way, since after each backward sweep, he will simply have to decide on whether to change towards the left or right side.

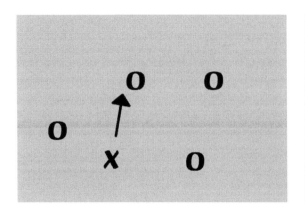 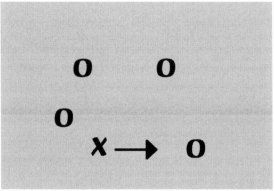

After pushing away the opponent on the left, the outnumbered combatant (x) has to read whether he should step towards the front / left or right.

Though outside of the scope of this introductory book, the development of combat skill for outnumbered scenarios also includes the following settings of higher complexity:

**Combat against five or more opponents,
Two combatants against a higher number of opponents,
Combat in restricted space,
Combat with traditional staffs that have blades fitted on the tip.**

The historical link to single combat

Some readers might find it strange that, in the photos presented, the outnumbered combatant was constantly attacking and never forced to parry. To the inexperienced eye, it might seem that the opponents are just passively allowing their opponent to move around, but that is not the case. As I explained in the main guidelines for engaging multiple opponents, initiating a strike from a distance where the opponent cannot be reached is of no use. Therefore, by standing still and luring the opponents to close the distance, outnumbered combatants can lead them to false assumptions, and take them by surprise with pre-emptive strikes as they are approaching. This means that, in "real" combat:

Sweeping an opponent's strike before following through with a counter attack (see also the two following spreads)

Special notes • 199

1) The first opponent who is attacked by the outnumbered combatant is usually taken by surprise and quite often, hit.

2) At the same time that the outnumbered combatant closes the distance towards that first opponent, he also increases his distance from the remaining opponents, who feel the need to get closer to their "victim" before initiating a strike. As they approach, the outnumbered combatant can use the same "trick" and inflict yet another pre-emptive strike that forces the multiple opponents to a defensive role.

Since outnumbered combatants can always rely on several different options available to them, they are able to continuously take the initiative and never relinquish it, thus relegating their opponents to defensive reactive roles. By pushing some opponents away while increasing the distance from the remaining ones, they can successfully use the same concept over and over again. Ultimately, this gives outnumbered combatants the advantage of not even having to deal with incoming strikes , as the opponents are constantly either parrying or out of striking distance, as a result of always being one step behind in this game of managing distance.

Of course, this will happen in an ideal situation, in which outnumbered combatants have good distance management skills and are also capable of swiftly moving in different directions as a result of proper body control. In reality, outnumbered combatants might find themselves finishing a strike against an opponent while another has managed to get closer than expected and is able to initiate a strike. When this happens, as I explained during the introduction of the sweep from above, outnumbered combatants are to continue their "normal" motion so as to sweep their opponent's strike with the first swing of the sweep from above. Given

outnumbered combatants' need to square off with opponents positioned in different directions, these half rotational parrying motions are, out of need, born out of backward pointing waiting guards, but doing so also ends up generating more than enough momentum to sweep through opponents' strikes. Consequently, they are designated as "in-motion parries".

This summary of the concepts previously presented is meant to support the explanation concerning the historical and technical evolution of combat skills which I will present in this section.

Historically, when people find themselves either in self defense situations or in the battlefield, without a doubt outnumbered combat is more

common than combat against a single opponent. People who live under the pressure of fighting for survival will, obviously, focus their training on the development of the skills required to succeed in this type of environment. One of those skills is the above mentioned in-motion sweeping parry performed from backward pointing waiting guards.

According to the concept known as the "Law of the Instrument" (expressed by Abraham Maslow in 1966) we tend to over-rely on an instrument that is familiar – if the only tool ones has is a hammer, he will treat everything as if it were a nail! I find this to be very true since, at one time or another, we are all confronted with problems that require an ideal set of skills we lack and, whenever this happens, we simply try to make do by adapting the skills we already possess.

In this sense, combatants who focused their training on developing the skills required for outnumbered combat, when occasionally involved in combat against one opponent, were forced to adapt, by making the best possible use of the skills they had. When combatants are only skilled in performing half-rotational swinging parries to intercept strikes from multiple opponents, upon facing a single opponent, they feel forced to use waiting guards that allow them to make use of these parrying techniques. This brought about the backward pointing waiting guards, where the weapon is held pointing backwards, either over the head or by one's hip.

Backward pointing waiting guard

As illustrated in the following group of photos, from these waiting guards combatants could react against full rotational strikes by sweeping them and following through with counter attacks.

Application of the sweeping in motion parries to single combat (see also following spread)

One thing must be noted though: It is quite hard to protect the legs when performing sweeping parries, so it is important to first step out of the opponent's reach during the parry, before following through with a counter attack. The reason is that, if combatants perform this type of parries without exiting when facing strikes randomly aimed at different heights, quite often they will fail to parry and in the absence of having distance as a backup, they will get hit on the legs.

Eventually, due to the Industrial Revolution, people moved from the countryside to the cities and the once pure martial practice for combat against multiple opponents forged in battlefields was gradually transformed into a leisure activity focused exclusively on combat against a single opponent. This type of practice brought about the creation of new techniques and strategies that allowed for greater effectiveness in this type of combat. In this context, the previously mentioned backward pointing waiting guards were replaced by other more fitting options.

This, my fellow martial arts enthusiasts, is how combat skill developed. Social and cultural conditions motivated trainees to adapt their practice so as to focus on the many different success criteria that varied over time. Additionally, as opponents' own abilities improved and, thus, made certain previously successful strategies obsolete, combatants were forced to devise new strategies and

techniques, a process known to most as EVOLUTION!

Ultimately, by having a better understanding of the circumstances which conditioned the development of each set of skills, combatants are able to perform better when sparring, since they are able to interpret and adapt more effectively to opponents showcasing different sets of skills and strategies.

Final notes

THOSE WHO KNOW ME either from attending my classes, training with me or simply getting together to talk and have some laughs, are well aware of both my passion for martial arts as well as my enthusiasm and eagerness to help others excel.

Having embraced these recent projects under this same motivation and dedication, I hope to have been able to convey in a straight forward and pleasant way these important concepts regarding an area of martial skill rarely trained, and which I also view as fundamental in developing a practical understanding of the historical and sociological constraints surrounding skill development in martial arts.

Obviously none of this would ever be possible without the sacrifices made by other instructors before me and their dedication to the art that helped preserve it through time. Personally, I find that Jogo do Pau is more than a "mere" living tradition with unbroken lineage, in the sense that it is a treasure we have been blessed with, both from a sociological standpoint and a martial skill perspective. It is a chest with many answers for those interested in interpreting and understanding the past, present and future of martial skills. Wouldn't it be funny if, some 500 years after the Portuguese set out to sea in order to give the world to the world, as eloquently described by renown Portuguese poet Luís de Camões, if the birth of a new martial paradigm would develop from this ancient, though almost forgotten, European combat system preserved by this once great nation?

In this sense, I feel that it is important to recall that Portugal had to fight for its independence, had to conquer new land by force so as to extend its territory, while also resisting the attempts made by its apparently stronger neighbor to conquer it again. I am not one to say we are the best, since I do not believe that anyone can claim that and, additionally, I also have a deep respect for many others who also achieved plenty of great military successes. However, credit should be given where it is due and, in this sense, we deserve a significant amount of credibility regarding our past military exploits and, more specifically, the combat arts on which they were supported.

Luís Franco Preto
August 2011

About the author

Luis Franco Preto has been training in martial arts for 25 years. Jogo do Pau has been the main focus of his practice and research for the past 16 years, He has served as technical director of The Portuguese jogo do Pau Federation for six years. After studying the art as it was systematized by the lifelong work of previous Masters such as Master Nuno Curvello Russo, he has focused on the enhancement of training methods. This process led him to acquire an undergraduate degree in Physical Education (Faculdade de Motricidade Humana) and two masters degrees, in sports teaching methodologies (Universidade Lusófona de Humanidades e Tecnologias) and in coaching sciences (University of British Columbia).

He has coached team sports and individual sports, as well as endurance athletes. However, over the years, his focus has been centered on the practical application of sports sciences towards the optimization of performance within martial arts and combat sports.

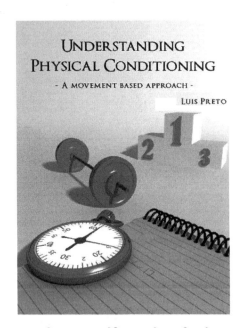

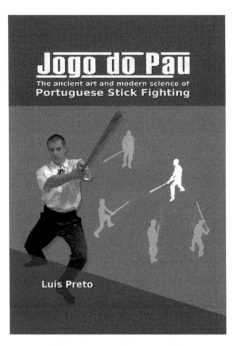

Understanding physical conditioning: A movement-based approach

"This book is aimed at martial artists who really want an educated approach to structuring their conditioning. Luis has done an amazing job of explaining not only the how, but why a martial artist should structure their conditioning using sound scientific methods and not the vagaries of exercise fashions".
– Paul Genge

Jogo do Pau: The ancient art & modern science of Portuguese stick fighting

"Luis does a phenomenal job of going over the basics of Jogo do Pau in both single and multiple opponent scenarios. I also learned much more about the history than I was expecting, and as a result I have an even greater appreciation for the art itself. Lastly, as an aspiring martial arts instructor, the section covering teaching martial arts had some advice and methodologies that I hadn't thought too much about, and find quite compelling".
– Ronald McKeehan Jr.

Fencing Martial Arts: How to sequence the teaching of technique and tactics

Staff, baton & longsword combat series: Functional parrying skill

"A great instructor is a treasure, but sadly one many cannot find. So, what is needed is help in self-instruction. Luis Preto's book offers the single greatest tool an instructor requires, he helps us find the right way to think about our task. There's so much more here, but that alone makes his book an irreplaceable text."
– *Pasquale Scopelliti*

"This book has a very simple purpose, to teach people about the fundamentals of parrying with hand held weapons and it does so in a very simple and direct way. Have you ever heard the expression, "You don't know what you don't know"? You would be surprised how many aspects of a functional parry there are that you wouldn't intuit on your own. Fortunately, now you don't need to. Luis Preto is the real deal; he knows his stuff and he knows how to teach it".
– *Michael Edelson*

 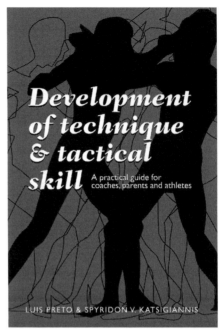

Staff, baton & longsword combat series: Understanding and developing footwork

"Luis Preto has mastered the techniques by which one can achieve maximum power in every strike by using the whole body's movement in the attack. His study of footwork is of extreme relevance to this subject, since it teaches the student to direct weight, strength and speed in the right direction, while making use of every single movement to achieve the highest possible degree of damage. His great teaching skills make this book absolutely essential for any martial artist".
– David Silva Ramalho

Development of technique & tactical skill A practical guide for teachers, parents and athletes

"...all coaching methods are not equal and all students are not at the same place in their development. By reading this book you will learn how to use most appropriate methods for the skill level of your students and then maximise the retention of their improved motor skills.
In short this is a book that I cannot recommend enough to anyone wanting to improve their coaching ability."
– Paul Genge

The Art of Riding on Every Saddle

This book written by D. Duarte, a fifteenth century Portuguese King, embodies in a very unique way the spirit of knighthood.

This is a result of D. Duarte's revolutionary way of approaching this art, by focusing both combat and horse-riding techniques on the person behind these skills.
Being a strong believer in the ability to improve one's character, D.

Duarte's lessons on will power, managing fear and being one with the environment, are as relevant for today's society, if not even more, as when they were written.

Thus, the precise and straight forward way used by D. Duarte to approach these psychological and spiritual topics make this book a valuable adviser for anyone looking to progress from Martial Artist to Instructor and, finally, becoming a Teacher.

D. Duarte's brilliant insights into the Human spirit are now available through this 2nd edition, which includes a NEW CHAPTER on recent research that raises intriguing questions regarding both identity of the portrait usually thought to be D. Henrique, Duarte's brother, as well as D. Duarte's own name.

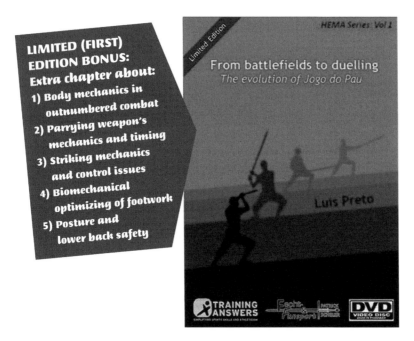

From battlefield to duelling: The evolution of Jogo do Pau

Jogo do Pau finds its roots on Europe's battlefields in the Portuguese long sword, the Montante, and was preserved to this day through staff fighting, in both duelling and outnumbered situations.

This noble, yet highly effective art is now made available to you, helping you to simultaneously improve your interpretation of historical European martial arts and your own combat skills.

Luís Preto, voted HEMA's 2012 instructor of the year, shares through this DVD a straight forward summary of his almost 20 years of experience in Jogo do Pau, in a unique case study that serves now as a valuable blueprint in the analysis of the evolution of combat tactics over time within HEMA, - From battlefields to duelling.

"The fundamentals discussed in this DVD provide an invaluable shortcut to all serious trainees, from beginners to advanced ones, seeking to learn from a historical, yet living martial art"

This DVD covers in five chapters how outnumbered combat influenced the first tactics used in single combat and its evolution, defining a combat logic for: • initial guard selection • assessing different defensive footwork options • counter attack choice at variable speed, body positioning and distance • striking options dependant on reach and defensive readiness.

Incl. numerous partner drills with comments read by HEMA instructor Roman Vučajnk and highlighted by detailed explanations and chapter summaries from Luís Preto.

Made in the USA
Middletown, DE
08 May 2015